Dear Carl -

The answers are found in a person

His name is Jesus

and

He loves You.

Hazel McAlister

NO PAT ANSWERS

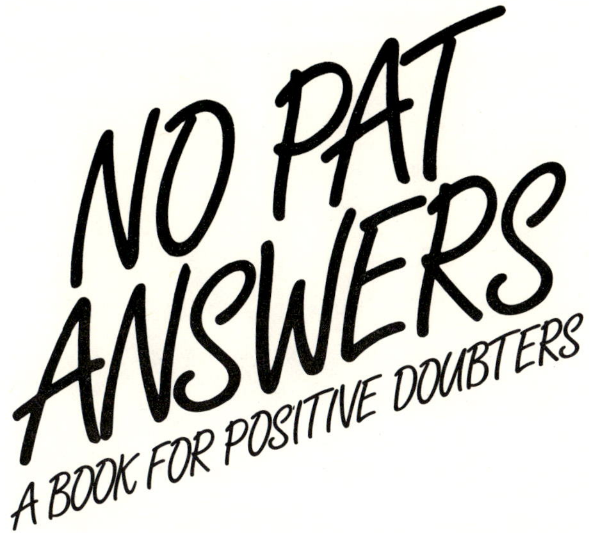

HAZEL McALISTER

ABINGDON PRESS
NASHVILLE

NO PAT ANSWERS

Library of Congress Cataloging-in-Publication Data

McAlister, Hazel.
No pat answers.
1. Christian Life—Meditations. I. Title.
BV4501.2.M4352 1986 242 85-28609

ISBN 0-687-28035-4

pbk.: alk. paper

Verses marked KJV are taken from the *King James Version.*

Verses marked AOT are taken from *The Amplified Old Testament*, copyright © Zondervan Publishing House, 1962.

Verses marked TLB are taken from *The Living Bible*, copyright © 1971 by Tyndale House Publishers, Wheaton, IL. Used by permission.

MANUFACTURED BY THE PARTHENON PRESS AT
NASHVILLE, TENNESSEE, UNITED STATES OF AMERICA

with gratitude to

Jack—

my husband of forty years
whose love encourages me
and makes me believe
that my writings have merit
and can help.

Dr. Daniel Brown—

whose red-pencil editing
demanded that I write
with clarity and honesty
and who refused to let me hide
behind useless jargon
and pious pap.

My thanks—

I am grateful to God
for both of you.

Contents

NO PAT ANSWERS

Introduction

I have tried to write
so that my words are not like
    a small, neatly tied parcel,
giving the impression
that the issues of our lives
    are equally small
    and easily tied up.
I have wanted to write something
    personal,
    realistic,
    pertinent,
to write of courage,
    strength,
    and perseverance
so that we may stride over
    our difficult places
    with confidence
    and even with joy.
I am always tempted
    to ignore unpleasant things,
    to see only what I'd like to see—
    in other words, be an ostrich!
But I have been compelled
    to write of complicated issues,
    matters that call for thought and discussion,
    that do not easily fit into the evangelical mold—

to offer you the love,
respect,
concern
in your problems that I want in mine.
And I am learning that truth
never damages Truth.
Yet when I realize that my writings
shout my secret thoughts for anyone to read,
I am afraid.
I dread the permanence of print!
But if I pick up my yellow pad and my mother's pencil
to write trite sayings,
religious jargon,
useless words,
I cannot take either you or me
into a deeper understanding
of the One who suffered
to make my suffering meaningful,
who provides freedom
that does more than free me
from pain, problems and suffering.
I know that life is filled with
disappointment and confusion,
mysteries and questions
to which there are no pat answers.
But I know, too, that the power
and presence of the living Christ are more than
adequate for moment-by-moment living.
He has walked with me
through the confusion,
hurt, and darkness
not so much providing answers to
my questions as being my friend
It's not that there are no answers,
but that answers aren't that important.

Beginning News

Change, change, change.
    Nothing will ever be the same again;
    we're moving—to a new home,
        new friends,
        a new ministry (whatever that will be).
I don't like it.
    I didn't want it,
but it's happening
and nothing will ever be the same again.
Change does not occur
    without fumbles in the dark,
    limps in our courage,
    and questions in our questions.
Every change is a chance
    for a new beginning.
To some, change brings new reluctance,
    reveals desperate feelings of insecurity,
    and faith as durable as a snowball in a jacuzzi.
To others, change brings a new desire to believe,
    a new urgency for faith—
    faith that rests in God's promises.
Too often we don't want to take responsibility for change,

or the new responsibility pressed upon us
by the change,
and so we resist.
Faced with the need to change,
some of us stop what we are doing,
never to begin anything again.
Change often brings death
to that which has gone before,
that which is old
the baffling excitement,
the disappointments of the old adventure,
the limitations of the past—
they are gone,
as irretrievable as shattered glass.
With change there is the promise of death
to anger that causes agony of soul,
to rancor and bitterness that lay waste our spirits,
to the monotonous hurts of emotional pain (rather than distress).
A friend of mine got a divorce
after much pain
and constant crying
because of a wretched marriage.
She told me, "When I signed the final divorce papers,
the pain was gone;
I died."
Now she was ready to live again.
Jesus once said:
"Except a corn of wheat fall into the ground
and die,
it abideth alone."*

**John 12:24* KJV

It too must change.
The more we die,
    the more God has a chance to live in us.
Jesus reacted the way we do—he didn't want to die.
He prayed not to change,
    for a way out of change.
With tears and supplications—he prayed,
"Oh God, if it be possible
    let this cup of change pass from me."
He changed by choice
that we might have the choice
to change.
He could have been a king.
He chose instead to be my Savior.

Taking off My Masks

It is not easy for me to say
that I need to come out from behind my mask,
my false face,
and phony
disguises
and admit to being human.
It's not bad, to be human;
it's good to be human.
The bad has been that I am afraid
to tell it,
afraid to admit
my humanness.
It is time to come out and say,
"I get distressed and disheartened.
Please help me.
I need someone to talk to,
someone I can trust,
someone who will listen
and not talk."
Let's put aside our subterfuge
and lay aside our deceptions.
Get honest with ourselves—
with each other,

with people, and
with God.
Perhaps the order should be reversed—
honesty with God first,
ourselves next,
and then
our family and friends.
I'd like to drop my cover,
take off the mask
that makes me look victorious
when I'm not,
the smile that masks
my social failures
and blunders.
I'm not perfect—far from it.
My blood flows red and easy like yours.
My wounds and scars are deep.
I often have a lump in my throat
and a hard knot in my stomach.
Tears are sometimes close to the surface
all covered up by the smile
that is my cover-up.
The careful observer can see that
my eyes are not smiling.
I get discouraged.
I have a difficult time handling my feelings.
When people ignore me,
disappoint me,
discuss my faults
and failures,
I harbor bitterness
and try to justify a nonforgiving attitude.

I would like to believe
I just took off my mask
    and stopped pretending,
but that is just another of many masks.
There is one mask that camouflages
the self-centered, self-pitying, self-love
    that festers in my heart,
    gnaws away at my soul,
    blinds me to the needs of my friends
    and damages my spirit.
I cannot ignore the one I wear
when I try to hide from God.
It could be a death mask
    made from fear
    and pride.
(Pride by any other name is fear—
they are the same.)
Fear that maybe God will embarrass me,
        expose my shortcomings for all the world to see,
        reveal my inability to leave my life in his hands,
        my tendency to work out my own destiny;
        my desire to help the Holy Spirit do his work;
        my constant need for reassurance;
        my refusal to trust;
and the pride I have in my own ability to live a good life.
O, GOD!
My reaction to all of that is revulsion—
I am afraid that it will be yours, too.
Even so,
I have to take off my masks,
breathe freely for a change.
PLEASE, God—HELP!
            I am suffocating.

Choices

I pulled the covers over my head,
burrowed down into my electric blanket.
Tried to ignore the fact that it was time to
get up
get dressed
have breakfast
talk to Jesus
read the Bible
clean the house
fix my face
and get moving toward a busy day.
    There is so much to do,
    so many people to talk to.
    Everyone clamors for attention.
    The telephone never stops ringing.
    There is so little time.
    We have just moved,
    and we aren't settled yet.
    Nothing is in place, and
    I'm only one person—
    one tired person
    trying to do the work of three people.
    I feel that I'm suffocating,

and I don't like it.
And so—I just lay there,
warmed and comforted by my electric blanket,
not wanting to face the onward rush
of a new day.
Sweetly, quietly the voice within spoke,
*Choose you this day whom ye will serve.**
"Lord," I replied, "I have chosen.
I have chosen you.
You are the one I serve."
Again—*Choose you this day whom ye will serve.*
With that,
God and I began another war,
though this time, maybe it was only a skirmish.
He pushed—I pulled.
He said, *yes*—I said, no.
He said, *You will*—I said, "I can't—
    I don't want to—I haven't even had my coffee,
    and I don't want to think."
I was exasperated: "LORD,
    I chose you a long time ago."
He persisted, *Today—choose today.*
The skirmish continued—but as always
God was winning,
and at last I heard him say—
Today—you can serve yourself
and your day will be as murky,
                                    as dull
                                    and rain-filled
                                    as the winter gray sky above you.
But—choose well this day, my child,
and serve me.

*Joshua 24:19 KJV

Your darkness will become light.
Your day will be filled with life—my life.
The mad scramble will be gone.
You will not be overburdened
by puffed-up nonsensical situations,
or overwhelmed
    with phantom problems.
You will finish your work.
Gloom will dissipate in MY light.
You will be warmed,
        comforted,
        and blanketed in MY love.
Get up, my child,
and face this day with high spirit
in the confident anticipation
that my unfailing,
      unfaltering peace,
      uninterrupted
      and unending joy
will be yours.

Be Perfect

This morning
    I tried to have the perfect hairstyle
    and
    burned my face with the curling iron.
    I wanted to have perfect fingernails,
                be a great cook
    and,
    while burning the breakfast bacon,
                broke a fingernail.
    I would like to be the perfect size,
    but
                thin is in.
    I can never be thin.
My complexion isn't perfect:
    my eyes are small,
    my nose is crooked,
    my lips are the wrong size,
    I cover the gray in my hair,
and my appearance is not perfect.
I would like to be perfect
and have
the perfect husband (he is better than most but he isn't quite),

children (they don't quite make it either),
the perfectly cared for home (I try, but I miss the mark);
so, how in this wide world
can I be perfect?
I realize these are unimportant imperfections.
My Christian faith, too, pushes me toward perfection.
In Corinthians Paul said: "Be perfect."*
The writer of Hebrews said, "Let us go on unto perfection."**
Yet the style of today is for perfection—
    perfect cars
        jobs
        bodies
        relationships
        marriages—
everything perfect.
So I try to be a perfect Christian (whatever that is)
    and fail,
        and fail,
            and fail.
I always fall far short
of my idea of perfection.

Then I realized there is a secret
to becoming perfect.
We get that way
    by reading God's word,
        walking in his ways,
        talking to him,
        listening, while he talks to us.

*II Corinthians 13:11 KJV
**Hebrews 6:1 KJV

I am so busy trying
to look perfect
act perfect
think perfect thoughts
have a perfect—everything,
there isn't enough time left over
to be with him.
Jesus tells us
to be perfect.
There are no perfect people!
And it hardly seems possible to become perfect.
But it must be.
We are never told to do impossible things.
He,
Jesus, my Lord,
is perfect.
I would like to be as he is.
But
the contrasts are unbelievable.
He is strong;
I am weak.
He is without fear;
I am often afraid.
He made himself of no reputation;
I protect mine.
He became a servant;
I want to be served.
He was kind to people who were unkind to him;
I try to ignore people who are unkind to me.
He prayed: "Father, forgive them."
I pray: "Father, forgive me. I don't want to forgive."
When people look at me they see pride,
damnable pride,
and I don't even know it's there.

And Jesus can't be seen.
How can I be as perfect as he?
I miss the mark on every point.
It's not easy to be like him.
He was the Rose of Sharon;
    I am just thorny.
He is wisdom;
    I am wise in hindsight.
He is light;
    I am dusky and dull.
He is the bread of life;
    I am frozen dough.
He is the lion of the tribe of Judah;
    I am only the roar.
He is the perfect Lamb of God;
    I am the balking goat
        or the braying ass.
He is the perfect Son of God;
    I am imperfect,
but—the big "but"—
he was chosen of God—and—so am I.
He lives in me.
I live because he is in me.
He is all my hope
    and my helper.
He covers
    my weaknesses,
        my faults,
            all my failings
with his righteous robe,
and—when
my heavenly father looks at me,
he sees me perfect
as his son is perfect.

Formulas Don't Work

Today was moving day.
The movers were five hours late.
They arrived hot,
tired,
and grouchy.
When they dragged reluctantly into our house,
we all wished they were someplace else.
When the furniture was finally moved
I was appalled;
dust was leering at me from every corner;
the empty places left by the pictures embarrassed me;
the garage cluttered and dirty,
it could hardly have been worse.
And all this junk,
who would want it?
I've worked so hard—my fingers hurt,
my nails broken,
and I've only cleaned one house.
I could hardly believe the way it looked,
and worse than that
the truth is out,
from under the refrigerator,
under the dresser,

and from every corner the leering dust.
My housekeeping isn't so great after all.
(Is my heart like my house, I wondered,
full of junk that I would be better without?)
One of my friends once called me Mrs. Clean.
I'm glad that friend isn't here now.
I taught a class, "Making Housework Easy."
"Take the drudgery out of cleaning," I said.
Organize.
Keep your house clean.
Don't let things get dirty.
Don't let anything get ahead of you.
Thoroughly clean one room each week.
Do one really difficult job every month.
Sort out.
Give away.
Throw away.
Don't be a pack rat
and a hoarder.
A messy house
indicates a messy heart.
Get your heart in order.
Get your priorities straight.
Clean up your emotional act
and you will clean up your house.
Today these are empty words.
Some days our formulas just don't work!
Those are the days
when I run
to the quiet place,
the secret place,
the place of promises (God's)
and remember for my comfort

Jesus tells us
that his plans are good
for our good,
and are not for evil.
Formulas are needful,
but formulas don't work for
the junk in our lives:
bitterness in the corners,
unforgiveness in the cupboards,
dust and cobwebs in our minds,
or the debris in the secret places of our hearts.
And so we trust, knowing
we don't need formulas.
We need Jesus.

The Day After

Right up its side
my pencil says "Joy of Living."
But I don't feel much joy in living now.
Yesterday was moving day.
So much work done to make so much work to do:
    boxes clamoring to be opened;
    empty closets waiting like caverns to be filled
with clothes in piles
on the bed or
in jumbled crumpled messes
on the floor
left—like junk—where the movers dumped them.
I hate moving.
Boxes all over the place,
    clutter and confusion
    every place I look.
I am exhausted.
I'll never get this confusing mix
of order and disorder
straightened out.
This morning when I got up
    I fell over the clothes that are heaped on the floor.
I walked into the unfamiliar kitchen
    with its half empty boxes and half full cupboards,
    everything in haphazard disarray.

I couldn't find the coffee—
    without my morning cup of calm—
    I wouldn't wake up,
    no one could talk to me;
what a disaster that would be.
When I walked through the disorder
that was my new home,
I had no joy.
But then I remembered Jesus
    specializes in new beginnings,
and promised us a new home where everything is in order.
He is not a joy-killer
    but a joy-giver.
Joy
does not come from a well-ordered,
        immaculate home,
nor is it found in my circumstances.
It is found in a person—Jesus—the giver of joy.
Moving is a horrendous experience.
It's late.
    I'm tired.
It's been a long,
        long day.
I'll dump this junk on the floor
and fall into bed.
I'll rest in the joy of the Lord
and next week when order is restored
and the house is as clean
as it looks,
and my mind is unstopped,
            uncluttered,
            and stayed on the Lord,
my joy will be full
again.

Consider This

The capitivating blonde,
    brown-eyed canine joy of two families,
let out of her yard
was needlessly killed
by a careless driver
on the busy streets of Los Angeles.
I, the first owner and self-appointed grandmother,
and Karen, the mother in the home
in which this rowdy,
            romping,
            fun-loving creature lived,
stood in tearful embrace
trying to comfort one another while
mixing their pain
with happy thoughts of a little dog
who had the marvelous capacity of lightening burdens
and provoking laughter
with her absurd and comical behavior.
The words of consolation would not come—
their grief blanketed them like a foggy cloud.
Tears flowed as they felt the pain
of losing the fun and frolic
Buffy so lovingly gave—to everyone.

Finally, the crying stopped.
I, the elder of the two,
    left to go home,
but in a moment I returned,
hoping to offer a few words
that would bring some token of comfort
to the children.
They would be so sad.
Adorable, happy little Buffy
hit by a car and
killed.
As I got into my car,
my heart was sad.
I thought about the tears,
                hurt,
and heartache I was feeling.
All—because a dog had died.
The lump in my throat
exploded into devastating tears,
so many tears, so much pain.
My heart was torn knowing
that I had not felt such pain
    for people—in the streets
    who go into eternity,
            lost
without knowing God's love
because I didn't care enough
    to bring them into
        the yard,
        God's yard,

before they died.

Her Heart Sees

Today I saw a lady
I will never forget—Ada;
    a full-grown lady,
blind from the moment she was born.
She has never seen the sun
    or the interesting things that we forget to look at.
She has never seen smiling babies,
                                        laughing children,
                                        or happy adults.
She cannot comprehend the brightness of this universe.
There are no shades
    and shadows in Ada's world,
only blank, dark nothingness.
Ada, a bright and shining light for God.
    A vibrant
        happy
        loving
        sensitive
        caring
        talented lady.
Beautiful—not as we know beauty.
But her soul,
    her spirit
captivating beyond anything eyes can see.

To God
she could be the most exquisite of all he created.
She doesn't care about
the petty
    unimportant
    prideful
    vain things
that tear us apart
and fill our lives with shadows.
For Ada
        the things,
        the places,
        and the faces of our world
don't matter.
They are unimportant
        Ugly
        unattractive
        unsightly—
these are words she doesn't understand.
She has never seen an *eyesore,*
                a spot,
                or a blemish.
She sees through the eyes
of her unpolluted,
    virtuous soul
and to her, every living,
        breathing thing is
alluring and enchanting.
"Don't feel sorry for me," Ada said.
"My first look will be at Heaven.
The first face that I will see
will be that of Jesus.
No, don't feel pity for me.
All I want to see is HIM."

Bridge for Two

A little boy, getting ready for bed,
interrupted a family gathering to say:
"I'm going to say my prayers now.
Anybody want anything?"

Sometimes I am like that:
I go to God with my shopping list
and expect him to feel honored
that I have taken time to "pray."
It is easy
    to pray
    as if God were room service
    or an errand boy
waiting to do our bidding.

Prayer isn't the grand mechanism
    we have made it out to be;
it is a bridge
    between ourselves and God.
Some of us put more faith in our prayers
    than in the God
to whom we speak in our prayers.
Some of us look at him as "the godfather"
rather than as the Father God,

and we think he isn't interested
in our prayers.
Some of us have given prayer so much importance and weight
it has become a burden.
If we didn't feel such guilt
about our lack of prayer,
we would pray more.
In prayer, what we say
is not as important
as what we feel-speak.
God knows what is in our hearts
and what we are trying to say,
even if we don't say it well.
Sometimes we make prayer like phoning,
and it's hard to get an operator.
The next time we talk to the Father,
let's dial direct—talk.
If we don't call,
he misses us.
He is waiting to hear our voices.
There really is something necessary about
this thing called prayer.
Not that everybody is doing it,
but a lot of people are asking for it—
friends
relatives
pastors
missionaries.
Even people who don't believe in prayer themselves—
friends and relatives, perhaps—
count on, ask for,
and depend on our prayers.

Do I Pray Enough?

Lord, why does such mystery
    surround this thing called prayer?
People write about it,
        talk about it,
        preach about it.
Sometimes I wonder if it's all talk.
Prayer is not something we will do.
It is something we have done
when we do it.
If I am to believe what the writers
                                talkers
                                preachers say,
I don't pray nearly enough.
Sometimes I feel such guilt
    I can hardly bear it.
I don't spend hours a day praying
    like the pray-ers say to do.
If I prayed more, I think,
    I would be a better writer
                            mother
                            wife
                            everything.

I pray on the run,
when I hurt,
when my son is sick,
when my daughter is having problems,
and when my mother died.
Are you saddened, Lord,
when I pray in bits and snatches
during the day?
Is it prayer
when I drive down the street
and thank you for the tree with the purple flowers,
or ask you to help the sad-faced man in the car next to me?
I know I prayed
the day my mother didn't know me
(only a few days before she had said:
"I'll never forget you, you're my Sally Sis"—
but she did forget).
I sat by her bed in the hospital crying, saying (maybe praying):
"Mother, where did you go, where are you?"
She couldn't answer me.
"O Lord," I cried, "please take care of my mother for me."
You must have heard me
when I asked for protection
on the long drive home.
You protected me from the other cars,
and the other cars from me.
And later when I fell across my bed sobbing and saying:
"Lord, please don't leave my mother like that.
Please, Lord, take her home."
That must have been praying
because you answered.

(You didn't seem to mind that I didn't get on my knees.)
Or in the morning
    sitting in the big chair,
    looking out the window,
    enjoying my coffee—waiting for the paper to come,
is it prayer when I say:
    "Thank you, Lord, for this day.
    Help me to please you,
    to be loving and kind like you are,
    and to love you more"?
Even if I don't hear your answer,
I know you are there
    enjoying my talking to you,
    loving me like my father did.
Then later
    when the lights are out,
    my family asleep,
    the house quiet,
and I am under my electric blanket,
I talk to you about my day.
Lord, remember the night I was so upset
because I had blown the whole day:
        I snapped at my daughter,
        talked through my teeth to my husband,
        got uptight with the salesclerk,
        had harsh words with Amy,
        was offended because I had been ignored,
        didn't like the empty nothing-letter I received—
that was a terrible night.
But I knew you understood
        and still loved me.
I relaxed and went to sleep.
That must have been prayer.

Maybe there isn't any mystery
    about this thing called prayer.
I don't need to feel such guilt.
    I pray more than I realize;
that is, if prayer
    is like two people
        who love each other
talking
        and being together.
Lord, I know that you love me.
Do you know that I love you?

God Listens to Me

When told he was going to have
a brother or sister,
a young boy asked his mother
if she had prayed for a baby.
When his mother said no,
he asked if his father had prayed for a baby.
When told no again,
he shrieked:
"Goodee! God listens to me!"

Many of us have an uncomfortable suspicion
 that almost everyone else
has a better prayer life than we do,
 and that God doesn't listen to us
  nearly so much
   as he does
    to the pastor,
    the saint down the street,
    the Bible class teacher,
    the television preacher,
    or even our good friend.
We recognize the importance of prayer;
we know it is a direct command.

"Pray without ceasing,"* the Bible says.
Our guilt about prayer
      periodically turns into a resolution
to develop a consistent
                    meaningful
prayer life.
But somehow the insistent
                      persistent
demands of everyday life
crowd out
                      the good intentions.
Prayer
gets only a little attention
                now and then.
Some of us think prayer is a duty.
Some of us pray only in extreme emergency.
To some, prayer is awkward
                              difficult
                              often embarrassing.
To some, prayer is abstract
      and not very meaningful—
we wonder if God listens to us.
To some, prayer is of great worth
and is the most meaningful thing they do.
They always find the time.
Sometimes when I go to God in prayer,
      I feel uneasy
                unsure
                uncomfortable.
I don't feel happy in his presence.
I don't want to be intimate with him.

*1 Thessalonians 5:17 KJV

I'm tired, and I'd rather go to bed.
I wonder if it isn't too simple just to ask God
why my mind refuses to clear itself,
or why I find prayer so demanding,
involved,
and sometimes so religious
and impersonal?
Why is there so much teaching on prayer?
When the disciples asked Jesus
to teach them to pray,
his answer was simple
brief
personal;
give us
forgive us
lead us
deliver us.
There were no limits
no contentions
no repetitions;
just a simple
sixty-nine-word, thirty-second prayer.
"Our Father which art in heaven,
Hallowed be thy name.
Thy kingdom come.
Thy will be done
in earth, as it is in heaven.
Give us this day our daily bread.
And forgive us our debts,
as we forgive our debtors.
And lead us not into temptation,
but deliver us from evil:
For thine is the kingdom, and the power,

and the glory, for ever. Amen." *
Sometimes when I am
face to face with the living God
I don't feel anything,
and leave my prayer life
to the mercy of my moods
because I am not prepared to receive
what he might give.
Instead of praying for the will of God,
I try to convince him to do my will.
In my struggle for a good prayer life (whatever that is)
my moods
my emotions
are irrelevant—
I don't always know what I am aiming at
or if he is listening.
The benefits of prayer are not found in
an emotional state,
nor are they governed
by my moods,
but they are found
when my believing becomes more believing,
my forgiving more forgiving
and my loving more loving,
and they are not found in a day
or in a week
or even in a month.
They are found as I believe God's word,
know that he is listening,
and continue to grow toward the time
when there will no longer be anything
in my life
to contradict my prayer.

*Matthew 6:9-13 KJV

Broken?

Child, you need to be broken, His voice whispered in my ear.
"Broken, Lord? I'm already broken.
How could anyone be more broken than I?
Lord, I am bruised. I hurt. I bleed.
Don't you know I am already broken?"
Again he whispered to my heart, *Child, you need to be broken.*
"But, Lord," I cried, "Don't you see I am already broken?
What does it mean to be broken?"
That question haunted me. As I pondered it,
I was perplexed because I knew I was already broken.
Again the Lord whispered to my heart.
Again, the answer, "Lord, I am broken."
Then with persistence,
Child, you are not broken; you only hurt.
If you were broken, as I was broken, you would not be hurting.
Your old nature woud not be crying; it would be dead.
Dead to yourself, your hurts, your dreams, your wishes, your earthly desires.
They would all be gone—all of them dead.
"Lord, how can I be broken like that?"
With gentle insistence, he again whispered into the quiet of my heart,
Child, you must come the way I did, the way of the Cross; it is the only way.

"The Cross, Lord? I've been to the Cross. I've been there with you."
Yes, child, but my body was broken for you.
His words, so familiar, rang out to challenge my understanding:
*This is my body, broken for you. Eat in remembrance of me.**
"Lord, that is just a symbol,
a token,
a ritual,
a ceremony to remember you by.
Your body is not recognizable
in those broken pieces of bread."
That's it, child. That is what I mean—be broken
until you are no longer recognizable
because you have been crushed
processed
refined
beyond all resemblance of your natural self.
Child, I let my Father break me,
and you must be broken, too,
broken until you think my thoughts
have my mind
live as I lived
want nothing
expect nothing
ask for nothing
forgiving all things and loving everyone.
My heart felt as though it were being torn from the inside.
Tears raced down my cheeks.
I convulsed with sobbing.
Finally—I knew—I had not been broken!
"Lord, break me as you see fit."

*See Luke 22:19.

Strain—A Melody

What a morning!
Nothing was going right.
My whole day had been sabotaged.
After weeks of dieting,
    depriving myself,
    going without,
I had lost five miserable little pounds,
    certainly not enough to show
        and make my new dress look good.
I wanted to chuck the whole thing.
It wasn't worth it;
Most people would have lost ten pounds.
"A slow metabolizer," the doctor said.
    It's hard for you to lose."
That's the truth.
The headaches,
    hunger pains,
    obsession about food
only added to my strain and misery.
I tried to remember
that
strain means either "excessive demands on one's emotions"
    or "the melody of a song."

Stress is "to pressure"
or "an accent in music."
We can choose the definition
that works best for us.
I would like the Holy Spirit
to help me hear life's melodies
accented with God's love,
instead of demands and pressures.
On the days
I am under galling strain
because of an empty refrigerator,
a house that isn't clean,
letters demanding answers,
bills screaming to be paid,
neglected devotional times,
and a diet that doesn't work,
I look at myself and know
it is easier to "unstrain" myself
if I get organized,
begin with the beginning.
Then I can spend my first few minutes in the morning with God,
and not go to him as a last resort.
If I ironed my clothes before I washed them—I'd laugh.
If I vacuumed the floor before I picked up the newspapers and glasses—you'd laugh.
If I took the dishes off the table before dinner
—my family would think I had finally cracked.
Or if I dressed in my good clothes to do the gardening
—I would think I had finally cracked.
Getting my priorities right
is as easy
as sweeping the floor before I scrub it.

When I give God the first hours of my day,
it is amazing how he—by his miracle power—
multiplies the hours,
adds to my talents,
increases my skills.
Because my spirit is quiet,
my attitude is peaceful,
my head is clear,
my thinking uncluttered,
the work goes easily.
The detestable defeats
of my ragged,
frazzled
days and hours are gone.
I finish what I begin
and no longer take unnecessary time
doing necessary things.
It is easy, then, to rest in peace,
walk in his love,
live what I say I believe,
sing songs of exaltation,
re-identify the words
stress and *strain,*
and remind myself they are
the parts of song.

Stress—An Antidote

It should be emphasized that
as long as we live
we are going to experience stress
and strain.
Pressures can become unbearable.
The refrigerator breaks down—food spoils—right after the warranty expires.
The dishwasher overflows—no one is home.
It's Christmas morning—the family is coming for
dinner—the sink stops up—(it really happened).
Guests are coming for dinner—you forgot to write it down.
You're going to a banquet for your husband's office—there is a spot on your best dress.
You dyed your hair—it turned henna.
Your new perm frizzed.
You spent the grocery money on a new dress.
It's time for church—there'is a run in your last pair of hose.
The puppy ate your husband's slippers—and got sick—just before company arrived.
You're late for the dentist—the kids used all the gas.

You burned a hole—in your husband's favorite shirt.
You lost the button that came off his best jacket.
Your daughter's new boyfriend lost his job.
These things only
show up my
    skimpy,
    imperfect ability
to keep myself stuck together.
The constant,
        unrelenting,
            oppressive stress
of everyday living
damages us
and our relationships with family,
                                        friends,
                                        and Lord.
Stress scrambles peace
    and makes sleep our best friend.
Frustration causes hearts to pound
                            and heads to ache.
Each of us handles stress in different ways.
    A minister I know reads a good mystery story.
    A friend does ceramics.
    Betty, my sister-in-law, makes gorgeous rugs.
    My mother knits teapot warmers.
    Another friend sews.
    Some people shop.
    I talk on the phone.
    These are all practical,
    easy things to do.
    If they don't work for you,
    one of the best things I know to do is—
    "throw a pillow."

Not long ago a good friend,
married for more than thirty years,
found herself in the middle of a dirty divorce.
She was haunted
by thoughts of suicide;
the pain almost destroyed her.
Her stress factor was at an all-time high.
She had heard all the pat answers—
"The pain isn't going to last forever."
"You'll be better off." (Ha!)
"He'll be back."
None of it worked.
The despair never quit.
One day, almost out of my desperation to help,
I said, "Throw a pillow."
"What do you mean?"
I replied: "Pick up a pillow.
Imagine your husband,
his girl friend,
the betrayal,
your agony,
all your fears,
the terrible aloneness
all rolled up in that pillow.
Throw it in the corner
and don't pick it up.
Every time you look at it, tell yourself
you are finished with those problems.
You might even give it a kick
once in a while.
It should help.
It works pretty well for me."
She did and it did!

Sometimes the pain is so bad,
the agony so all-consuming,
that you can't pray
or even think,
much less read your Bible.
The pat answers just don't work.
You can't be rational—
you can only pick up a pillow
and throw it in the corner.
And it's OK;
God really doesn't mind.
He understands.
Knowing that—
we can feel safe enough
and free enough
to be honest with him about our problems
and our feelings,
knowing stressful situations
are limited in effect because
our Heavenly Father
controls the events of our lives, and
he is never taken by surprise.

Victory?

Victory?
Is it really victory when anything
and everything we have prayed for
has been given to us?
"I was sick—I prayed—I was healed.
I had a miracle. God gave the victory."
Did he? I wonder.
"I needed money—I prayed—the money arrived.
God gave the victory."
Did he? I wonder.
"I had a personal problem—I prayed—the problem was solved.
What a miracle! God gave the victory."
Did he? I wonder.
I've heard testimony after testimony—
and they end—
"God gave the victory. He is the miracle worker."
Do we believe God has given victory
because we use him as our "answer man"?
If Jesus grants my requests,
    answers my questions,
    solves my problems,

am I his
or is
he mine?
I state the problem;
he must fit my solution.
He is not an experience,
            a solution,
            an answer man
            who wants to cheer me up
            and make me feel good.
He is my Lord.
He is my life.
Everything I have is in him.
He wants me to mature—
into a responsible,
        responsive,
        adult Christian.
Could it be
that in some of life's difficult,
                          trying,
                          even desperate times
he has responded to us as if we were babies
                                    and pacified us—
and we call it victory?
He gave us what we asked for—because
he couldn't trust us enough
to believe,
to rely on,
to follow him
if he didn't do what we asked.
If we are sick and not healed,
but still we continue our trust,
believing that Romans 8:28 is in the book

and true,
isn't that real victory?
If I am persecuted—left alone—
    in trouble—on every side,
but I say like Job:
"Though he slay me, yet will I trust in him,"*
isn't that victory?
If I have lost my job,
    can't find work,
    use up all my money,
    can't pay the rent,
    the lights and telephone are turned off
    the gas tank is empty
    the cupboards are almost as empty as I am,
and I feel like my name is Mrs. Job.
I am struggling,
    asking God if he knows my name
        and where I live,
but again, like Job, I say,
"Though he slay me, I will trust him."
Isn't that victory?
If this perplexing adventure
called life
has turned against you,
    you are pressed against an invisible wall,
    the dreams and plans of many years snatched away;
    your enemies outnumber your friends;
    you want to scream out against injustice and inequality,
    and everything within you says run,

*Job 13:15 KJV

but—you stay—impoverished and depleted,
    begging your heart to slow down,
accepting life as it is,
not giving in to despair
because you remember that Paul said,
"Stand fast in the Lord,"*
and you stand,
knowing that tomorrow is in
his hands,
and you are in his care—
isn't that victory?

*Philippians 4:1 KJV

Victory!

Victory is mine
when I accept with gladness
and thanksgiving
the lonely,
crushing depression I feel
when my friends leave me alone,
misunderstand me,
falsely accuse me
and judge me wrongly.
If I do not retaliate and try to get even,
I am no longer dejected and forlorn—but positive and hopeful.
Anger and bitterness melt—and I feel hot tears of contrition.
Depression evaporates—and I know the joy of reaching out.
The hard shell around me softens—and I become less selfish;
I am enjoying victory.
Victory comes when I
live in confidence that . . . God's thoughts for me are for good and not evil.*
When I confront opposition,
face rumor,
make difficult decisions

*See Jeremiah 29:11.

in the loving spirit of Christ—
that is victory.
When I please him in everyday things:
keep the shirts ironed,
bills paid,
checkbook balanced,
meals on time
and always have ice cream in the freezer for my husband,
and my ultimate goal in life
is to please God regardless of cost
circumstance,
inconvenience,
or pain—
that is victory.
When my faith is unwavering,
my believing unshakable
and I am not looking for
quick answers,
easy solutions—
that is victory.
When I forgive those who have
abused my friendship—
used it to their own gain—
betrayed my confidence—
and brought confusion into my life—
that is victory.
A lengthy and arduous trial—
the kind the Bible calls
"the trial of your faith, being
much more precious than of gold"—*

*I Peter 1:7 KJV

as, for instance,
an extended illness
or a period of financial distress
can become a time to become better acquainted with the one who makes victory possible—
to know his voice
feel his presence
recognize his hand touching my life
when he comes to comfort,
lead,
chastise,
and to love.
To be able to say
"Father,
if this affliction
has no distress,
no surprise, for you,
it has no doubt,
no fear for me"—
that is to know victory.
Many things that we think are victory
are merely the pleasant happenings of life.
Jesus—willingly nailed to the cross,
suffering three days in the grave and in hell,
voluntarily giving his life for me—
resurrected, to give again,
again
and again—
that—was the ultimate,
supreme,
peerless,
final victory.
My victory is not my own.
It is his, for he is my victory.

Green Skies

The loss of a dream.
    The death of a vision.
        The demise of ministry!
Such a defeat rips our lives like a tornado,
obliterating the sun,
    uprooting the trees,
        shaking and rattling foundations.
When a tornado is on the way
the sky turns green,
and you wonder if your skies will ever be blue again.
In tornado time,
people
run for cover.
When our tornado hit,
many of our friends ran for cover.
But, Lord, there are those who stay,
those special ones you send.
They love—they pray—
they care—they comfort—
they weep—they wipe tears.
And our family (thank you, God, for families)
closed ranks around us.
We are not alone.

And then one glorious day,
    we realized—that behind the green—the blue was still in our sky.
It was only hidden from our view.
We saw that the foundation
on which we had built our lives,
our relationship with Christ,
    held fast
        secure
        intact.
It did not quiver
    or shake in the tornado.
Again, we declare
that he is a faithful God.
His word is true.
Romans 8:28 is in the book:
" . . . all things work together for good
to them that love God. . . . "
He is the God who does not change.
    He cannot,
    he will not,
    he does not fail.
We can trust him,
    the unchangeable,
        unshakable,
        uncompromising God,
the one who promised:
"I am the Lord, I change not."*

*Malachi 3:6 KJV

Some Time Later

My thoughts,
    reflecting inner peace
        and tranquility,
    are pleasurable,
        warm, and comforting
as I watch the early-morning haze
lift from the hills that surround our home.
The tornado has ceased its furious blowing.
    Our skies—are blue again.
    The clouds—like huge cotton balls—hang in the sky.
    The wind—gently, quietly blows away the summer
    haze,
    The rains—cool, refreshing, and cleansing.
I lean back in my husband's big orange chair,
        close my eyes,
and gently say:
    "Father, thank you.
    You do everything perfectly.
    You are on my side!
    You are my friend!
You care about me
and will always take into account
that I am weak and frail.

When you take away something I value
or ask me to give up something,
you give me a treasure
    more worthwhile.
Life is not just a game of hide and seek.
    You did not hide yourself from me.
You went ahead and marked the path
that I should follow.
I found it in your book,
    I listened to your voice
    saying,
    Not this path;
    turn right here.
    No, not this corner, the next one.
    There, that's it—go straight ahead from here.
    You'll be happy here;
        it's the right place for you.
    My words are pale understatements
    of all you are
    and what you have done.
    "Lord, thank you for being my good friend.
        Today I want to know my weakness so that I may
            experience your strength,
        sure not of myself—but of you,
    I will put everything in your hands,
        knowing that you will not let me fall.
    Lord, I am grateful;
        make me more grateful still."

Don't Swim Against the Stream

Life was coming together
for the first time
in a long while.
The family was exceptionally sane.
I could look in the mirror without feeling fat.
My panty hose fit.
I had more than one dress that would zip.
My fingernails had grown long and lovely.
The house seemed to stay clean.
I had stopped eating cookies in the car,
chocolates in the bathroom,
and no longer needed to hide.
I was experiencing victory (the circumstantial kind),
the exhilarating joy of knowing . . .
all is well,
life is good,
the sky is blue,
the grass is green,
and God is smiling at you.
It was a great feeling!
And then . . .
a telephone call—
another difficult situation.

I was sandwiched between the panic and the problem.
My victory, like Humpty Dumpty, fell off the wall
and shattered.
The doctor's news about Jack's health was unexpected,
unreal,
unbelievable.
I wanted to break a window,
throw dishes,
scream insults
against this latest assault.
I was almost devastated—
almost—but not quite
because I do know,
even when I am not experiencing apparent victory
and the happenings of my life are hard to understand or
difficult to handle
and I feel like a pillar of marshmallows,
I'm really not out of victory
or out of God's will for me.
I know that God is in control
of all the nights
and of all the frights
in my life.
It's just that I can't feel it.
The changes on our lives in the last year
have been epoch making . . . almost catastrophic.
Our life is very different.
Now this.
My husband—a good man,
called of God,
anointed by the Holy Spirit,
has been ill for many months.
The illness could not be diagnosed.

The best doctors we could find,
the latest, most sophisticated medical tests,
were not able to determine what had caused
many months of night sweats,
loss of appetite,
a continuing high temperature,
three liters of fluid removed from one lung.
A man who has never smoked in his whole life
with lung problems—
unbelievable,
hardly possible,
yet it happened!
"It's enough, God," I told him.
"I've had enough problems
to last for four generations—
What are you trying to do,
grind us into dust?
Turn me into powder?"
I knew that was not the plan of a loving, caring Father God.
None of the pat answers fit this episode
of our upside-down world.
Any wrongdoing had long since been confessed
and forgotten.
Sin,
disobedience,
rebellion,
sullen reluctance to accept his plans—
we could find none of that.
The experience of daily forgiveness is ours.
Even so, we wondered about this undiagnosed illness.
We asked

questioned
and tried to ferret out any reason
causing this.
God's answer to us never changed:
You have entrusted your life to me.
I am not surprised by this;
I am totally involved in it.
My plan is unique:
walk with me,
talk with me,
get to know me better,
learn to follow,
and you will not be surprised by my ways.
You are in my hands
I know where I am taking you.
TRUST ME.
I know how many hairs are on your head.
I care about sparrows.
My care for you
is deliberate,
unconditional,
and trustworthy.
It is established forever—never worry!
Then this morning the call came from the doctor.
Of course,
I worried.
"Your husband has tuberculosis."
For just a minute (or maybe it was thirty or forty)
more panic
more questions
more confusion.
Then the still small voice spoke in my heart:

I am in control.
I know what I am doing;
trust me,
walk with me.
A difficult situation
    that lines up with my plans
is better than an easy situation
    that is contrary to my plans.
Do not swim against the stream;
    quit thrashing around looking for a wave to grab onto
    or a life jacket that is always out of reach.
All you need to do
    is to reach out,
        take my hand,
            rest in my care,
                feel my love,
have the grace to willingly,
                    eagerly,
                    lovingly,
                    embrace my will.
I am not ignorant of the effect
this has on your lives.
Do not misinterpret my dealings with you.
I am preparing you to live in
my house forever.

To Jack—With Love

The wind screams a protest,
the thunder rolls
and lightning skitters across
the early morning sky.
Rain pours in sheets of clear crystal,
washing away the dirt
                                  and debris
of the past.
The beauty is awesome.
The dark of night
and the eerie light of dawn
are locked
in mortal combat.
With fierce tenacity,
the dying night
pits herself
against the encroaching fingers
of dawn
that sound out the coming of the
fast-approaching light.
The trees,
      bushes,

flowers,
leaves
huddle
within themselves,
wrapped in the chilling misery
of the early winter rain,
vainly trying to protect themselves
against the relentless beating.
Beside the window, inside my home,
I stand protected
and warm,
secure in peace and calm,
knowing
that furious wind,
flashing lightning,
chilling rain,
or the roar of toothless thunder
cannot touch
or harm
me.
Emotionally,
spiritually,
I am
sheltered in God's arms,
protected in his love,
and encompassed with his presence.
No storm can harm me.
Off in the distance,
I see a stately palm tree,
in Bible times
used as "an instrument of praise."
As I watch,

an ugly,
    brown,
    decaying,
    dead branch
drops
and silently,
        slowly fades away,
and then another
    and another
until there is nothing left
but the lush green
of the seasoned
    living branches.
I imagine that the tree—
    stronger,
    immovable,
and unshakable in the storm—
    more stalwart now than before—
    smiles, knowing
that the harsh winds of adversity
only make the tree flourish,
give it great strength
and character.
The wind, unabated, continues
its savage beating.
The palm tree smiles again,
secure,
knowing
that the Creator is in control of all storms;
affliction and distress
will never break its back.
It will only knock off
    the useless,

dead branches
and its roots will grow deeper,
its character stronger.
Then the palm disappears from my view
I see you—silhouetted in lonely splendor against the sky.
I remember—dear husband—
who the psalmist likens to a palm tree:
"The [uncompromisingly] righteous shall flourish
like the palm tree [be long-lived, stately,
upright, useful and fruitful]; he shall grow
like a cedar in Lebanon [majestic, stable,
durable and incorruptible].*
—God has made you to be a strong palm tree.

*Psalm 92:12 *AOT*

Random Thoughts

Difficult situations
are magnified
by tension and fear.

All of us who are alive
are witnesses to
grief and glory.

Never get involved in the vicious game
some people play,
    selling themselves,
    their principles, and their ideals
for a mess of pottage
or
the pleasures of the moment.

If we are phony,
people will see right through us
to our true natures.

Don't be intimidated
by complicated, unfamiliar situations.
If we act with careful understanding
and show God's love,
we can be confident that
we bring pleasure to his heart
and immeasurable joy to our own.

God wants his children to have his best.
Some of us don't want his best;
therefore,
he can't give it to us.

A victorious, happy Christian is one
who knows that
God cannot make a mistake—regardless of how it looks.
A defeated, unhappy Christian
is one who thinks
God can,
and already has,
made a mistake.

Much of the unhappiness and confusion
in this world occurs
because we do not recognize
how little we need.

For spiritual growth,
some people don't need a pat on the back;
they need a kick in the pants.

I choose not to take hold
of the things
that would wet-blanket me.

Faith

Lean on the Lord.
Be confident in him.
Don't be supported by your own ability
to reason.
In every important decision,
act
as though you know him,
and he will
keep you going in the
right direction.*

*See Proverbs 3:5-6.

The world is full of people
who bluff
their way through life.

Set your own pace
and refuse to live at the pace
others set for you.

Strange
that in our praying
we seldom ask for a change of character,
but frequently for
a change of circumstances.

THE Lord is my shepherd.
The *LORD* is my shepherd.
The Lord *IS* my shepherd.
The Lord is *MY* shepherd.
The Lord is my *SHEPHERD.**

*Based on *The Shepherd's Psalm* by F. B. Meyer, Zondervan Publishing House, 1953.

Prayer

Some days it is easy to be loving,
to be kind,
and to trust—
Today is not one of those days.
Father, help me today
to be like your Son.
His name is
Jesus.
Amen.

It is so easy to tear down.
Why is it so difficult to build up?
Lord, help me to be a builder.

Gossip the love and power of Jesus.

Life can only be understood backward,
but
it must be lived forward.

Forgiveness should never be a one-time event;
it must be a life-style.

God said: "I want you to come and live
in my house forever.
But to feel at home there, one of us must change.
I am the Lord, I change not."*

God is calling his children to
holy living.
We cannot make ourselves holy.
But we can put off
those things that prevent
his holiness from
being evident in us.

*Malachi 3:6 KJV

Days of Doubt

I envy people who are always sure
of what they believe
and are not encumbered and pressed
by problems of skepticism
                    and distrust—
people who have not embarked on the long,
      trouble-ridden guilt trips
caused by doubt.
There are times when it is easy to
have trust,
        faith,
        confidence,
and reliance on God.
But—there are other times
when doubt clings
like a death-shroud
      to the good things
      God is constantly doing
      —for me,
      —to me,
      —in me,
      —and around me.

These are the times that
I cannot believe,
and I am not always sure that God is in control
    of the mundane,
        everyday
        happenings of my life.
So many things run amok
that sometimes I feel as if my roller coaster
is not only out of control
but also off the track.
My faith is like cotton candy,
useless in the wind and rain.
And then,
there are days when it's easy
    to trust the Father's ways
and not ask, "Why?"
Today is not an easy day.
I talked to him this morning
and wasn't sure I was making sense,
        or if he was listening.
        I doubted his reality.
I could find him nowhere.
Yesterday, though, I talked to him,
        read his word—and was fed,
        encouraged,
        enlightened,
        and lightened.
His presence was so incredible
I wanted to reach out and touch him
and never let him go.
Surrounded by his love,
    enveloped by his peace,
        overwhelmed by his calm,

I felt, well, covered.
He insulated me from feelings of inadequacy
and from the despair that is the
constant companion
  and friend of doubt.
Today, I feel so gone away;
  my Bible is lifeless and meaningless,
  my praying, empty and powerless.
I doubt his existence
and question his forgiveness.
Fear, quietly and subtly
disguised as doubt,
surrounds me.
Its murkiness grips my mind;
       it grabs my trembling stomach
       and presses it into a hard ball.
Fear's fingers fasten themselves
like barnacles
around my heart, and I listen
  to the emptiness
that threatens to swallow me.
Life is squeezing life out of me.
I long to believe.

Thomas, Me and You

How like the disciple Thomas I am.
    I have walked many miles with Jesus,
    talked with him often.
It is as though I've seen his face,
                felt his presence,
                experienced his love,
                tasted his joy,
and yet,
I still say, "Let me touch your hand,
                    feel your side,
                    hear your voice,
                    and then I'll believe."
I am so ashamed—my doubts leave me stranded.
My fermenting fears have caused me to lose sight of
    the hands I have touched,
    the side I have felt,
    the voice I have heard
of Jesus and his love.
I long to believe,
    and believe,
    and believe.
I wonder if Thomas, like me,
really longed to believe?

Was his desire, like mine,
so strong,
so dynamic
that he had to ask?
I'm like that,
    my mind full of doubts,
    my heart questioning and afraid,
all the time silently screaming,
"I want to believe,
Lord—help—
    help my unbelief!"
Is he displeased—
when I question his absence
    and wonder about his love?
Is he saddened
because, in puzzled desperation, sometimes
I have to say, "Lord,
    show me your hands;
    help me to believe"?
Does he understand
    that my deep,
        urgent desire
is to believe,
and that if I did not doubt
            I would not ask
            and could not learn
            and would never know
that he really is the Son of God.
Rather than unbelief,
doubt is a burning desire
        to be convinced,
        to believe,

to see,
to experience,
and to know
that he is always with me.
Lord, help me to be like
Thomas—convinced
because
I have touched
and seen
the resurrected Christ.

Positive Doubt

Never negate doubt.
It is a positive aspect of faith.
If we don't doubt,
        we don't ask.
If we don't ask,
        we don't get answers.
Thomas doubted.
He asked questions;
      he got answers;
and he believed.
It is not so with some of us.
We are afraid to doubt,
                    to ask,
                    to reveal weakness
                    and skimpy faith (even to ourselves).
We think God might not know
that we have a difficult time
believing;
so, we are ashamed to tell him.
He understands
that we all have doubt-filled times,
blinding us
                to his reality

and commitment to us.
His never-failing love can't be seen.
Admitting doubt is only
admitting humanity.
When I deny my doubts,
pretend to have all the answers,
and never question my ability to believe,
I fool myself.
Some days I'm full of faith
and it is easy to trust,
and I find little to offer the
doubting process.
Today, it is difficult to trust.
My faith got up and left.
God seems so far away.
His words are empty;
they have no meaning.
I wonder if any of them are true,
or if it is all just a bad joke.
I feel that God—if he is—
must surely want me to be miserable,
or I would not be full
of tormenting doubts.
I know he has no care for me!
In the middle of last night,
I was bombarded;
my doubting almost smothered me.
Sleep was impossible—
I imagined my son in a hospital and never coming home,
my daughter far from home and someone abusing her,
my huband in an airplane accident,
myself old and alone—

and God fast asleep!
Ridiculous! Yet not more ridiculous
than thinking God loves my brother better than he does
me.
Or—that God doesn't listen when I pray.
Or—that God listens only when you pray.
Or—that he uses my husband but he won't use me.
Or—that I am a no-talent person
and he merely tolerates me.
I'm so like Thomas, the disciple,
who asked to *see* for himself.*
Or like David, who asked for a token.**
Or Gideon, who put out a fleece.***
Someone once said:
"It is all right to doubt
if it brings you to Christ."
My doubt
is not unbelief;
it is an urgent desire
to know Christ better,
and believe,
and believe,
and believe.

*See John 20:25.

**See Psalm 86:17.

***See Judges 6:36-40.

Why, God, Why?

Why, God, why?
Tell me why
your children suffer so.
Living can be such agony,
often full of burning pain
    and unalleviated loneliness.
Lord, is that the ultimate—
dying so that the world can see
the brilliance of all you created?
Nature's births spring
    fragrant,
    flamboyant,
vibrating into summer
with colored majesty,
quietly breathing its last
adorned in the splendor of fall.
If dying is a part of living,
why must dying
be so impossible to live through?
Why, God? Why, in life's winter,
does it sometimes seem that
adversity has unleashed its furies,

snatching away our sleep,
and stealing our peace?
Lord, we are your creation, too,
uniquely fashioned by you
for enthusiastic,
abundant living.
Is that what you have planned for us—
a gentle spring,
a bright-flowering summer,
the radiant hues of fall,
and a blanket of glowing white for winter?
Then why, God,
are your children
bent by trouble,
hounded by difficulty,
buried beneath tons of debris,
barely able to exist?
Are we not your creation, too?
You must wonder, God,
why we keep *whying,*
waiting for answers
that will not matter on
the other side of here.

No Pat Answers

All of us ask
at some time in our lives:
"Why, God, why?"
I've discovered
there are no pat answers.
Your pain, my pain, is caused
by totally different circumstances.
  The eighty-one-year-old lady (my mother)
  had
  served God in magnificent fashion for seventy-five years.
  She stood beside the body of her eldest son
  and cried with agony of heart,
  "Why, God, why not me?
  I'm old, I'm tired.
  My life is full.
  Why, God, why?"
I couldn't answer her.
  Or the graduate student
  living in a room behind a garage.
  He has been jilted, his heart broken.
  Bereft in aloneness,
  the pain excruciating,

he cries; "Where is the God of my childhood,
the One who made everything right!
I'm so alone.
Why, God, why?"
I don't know the answer.
Or my friend—a widow—
whose daughter found life
too much and asked for less
in suicide.
She, too, cries;
"Why, God, why?
Where were you when my daughter needed you?"
I could find no answer.
Or the woman of distinction
who has it made in business.
She loves and serves God with all her heart
and longs for the right husband.
She prays.
She waits.
She cries,
"Where is the man you designed for me?
Why, God, why
am I alone?"
I can't tell her.
And then, my special friends
who—after giving themselves to God
in preparation for missionary service—
lost everything in a fire.
They, too, asked,
"Why, God, why?"
There didn't seem to be an answer.
Many of us have friends
with broken marriages and ruined lives,

whose businesses are broke,
lives are bankrupt,
babies are raising babies—alone.
Parents whose teenagers
become strangers,
leave home,
become drug addicts,
turn to alcohol.
These are just a few of life's situations
that many of us share.
In such times as these
we
feel abandoned,
destitute,
distraught,
and alone.
"God," we pray,
"why have you forsaken us?"
And then we remember that someone else,
in agony of heart,
has already prayed that prayer.
"My God, my God, why have you
forsaken me?"*
He didn't get an answer
before he died . . .

*Matthew 27:46 TLB

What Is the End?
or
A Three-letter Word

"Why, God, why?
Why this pain?
Why these frustrations?
Why these disappointments?
Why, God, why?"
These words have followed me into troubled sleep,
given me nightmarish days
and horror-filled dreams.
And the answers—my answers—
filled me with pain and misery,
caused my anguished heart and aching head
to rob me of the joy of early spring,
the contentment of summer evenings,
and the exciting energy of frosty winter nights.
"Why, God, why?"
My answers were always the same:
he doesn't love me;
he doesn't care about me;
he isn't feeling my pain;
he has forgotten where I live;
he probably doesn't even know my name.

"Why, God, why?"
    The words roar like thunder in my ears.
"Why? Why? Why?"
A three-letter word
to question the ruler of the universe.
How absurd
to question him,
    the Almighty God,
    the One Above All Kings,
    and the Leader of Lords.
Then one day in a quiet place
a friend, who also had known heart-wrenching pain,
    has cried in the darkness of her night
    until her eyes were empty
    and her tears all gone,
said, "Forget the why . . .
    it is of little use,
    it really doesn't matter,
    it only adds to your confusion
    and separates you from God.
Ask the question of love.
Ask the question of trust and acceptance.
Ask the question that heals.
    What is the end, Lord?
    To what purpose is this pain?
    What do you want me to learn?
    What are you trying to teach me?
    What good can come to others?"
When I did that, I found his answers
already given—I just hadn't heard them.
James said it:
"Dear brothers,
is your life full of difficulties
    and temptations?

Then be happy,
for when the way is rough,
your patience
has a chance to grow.
So let it grow,
and don't try to squirm
out of your problems.
For when your patience is finally
in full bloom,
then you will be ready for anything,
strong in character,
full and complete.*
Paul said it:
These troubles
and sufferings
of ours are, after all,
quite small
and won't last very long.
Yet this short time
of distress
will result in God's richest blessing
upon us
forever and ever!**
When I let those answers speak to me,
I remembered that I already knew
God does love me.
He does care for me.
He is feeling my pain.
"Forgive me, Lord.
You have called me.
You know my name
and you do care."

*James 1:2-4 TLB

**II Corinthians 4:17 TLB

Joy?

Joy and happiness are not abnormal emotions,
but talking to some people makes us
inclined to think they are.
I wonder if everyone is bewildered
by the complexity of life,
    by heavy burdens,
    and by hearts that are broken and oppressed.
Is God indifferent
to the unfruitful,
        depressing
        barrenness
that some of us live in?
Most people,
at some time,
bite and chew dust all day long
and have at least one problem
serious enough
to keep them floundering and
    feeling lost,
no longer feeling,
            believing in,
            or living in joy.

Joy comes with a deep,
lasting belief
that God controls
every circumstance.
James says
that we should consider it joy
when we fall into depression
and temptations
and we should know that
the test of our faith
cultivates patience.*
Happiness is easy
when life is smiling
and everything we hope for—
and more—happens.
But—when we are drifting along,
barely existing,
embroiled in situations that keep us
constantly panicked—
what then?
Our only hope is to experience
God's joy.
I was amazed not long ago,
listening to my friend Mary
talk about joy.
She was broke,
out of work,
her heart misbehaving,
the rent almost due,
and her former employer
giving her a bad time
about severance pay and

*See James 1:2-3.

unemployment insurance.
There was a difficult time
when Mary lost her control
and shattered into tiny pieces.
She then did what some of us do:
doubted,
questioned,
kicked,
screamed against injustice,
and knew God didn't care.
This time was different.
Concerned,
apprehensive,
mystified—
she was all of that,
but predominant in her thinking
and feeling
was the knowledge
that she served,
loved,
followed,
and worshiped a faithful God
who even allowed his son
to die—so she could know joy in hard places.
She knew, too,
that joy doesn't come from circumstances;
it is permanent
and can survive crisis.
The joy of the Lord enriches
without sorrow.

If we know his word,
    walk as he directs,
joy can be ours.
He knew we would suffer—as sheep among wolves,
        be disappointed—in our lives,
        feel hostility—in an unfriendly world,
        be afraid—of what is ahead,
but—he promised us joy.
    Gloomy faces,
    cheerless dispositions,
    morose, poisoned personalities,
    melancholy children,
    grumpy men,
    fearful women,
    down-in-the-mouth Christians
ought to be abnormal.
BUT ARE WE?
Perhaps we are fledgling followers
who are not aware
that Jesus set the pattern
for our joy
when he "sang a song"*
the night he gave his life
and paid a ransom
so that we might have everlasting joy.

*See Mark 14:26.

Joy!

Everyone wants to be happy.
Everyone wants to experience joy.
It is difficult to remember
that joy and happiness are different emotions
    and come from different things.
Happiness is fleeting,
        temporary,
and usually hinged to our circumstances.
  Joy is lasting,
      durable,
      permanent,
and is supported by our communication
            and companionship
with an infallible God.
The psalmist said: "Thou wilt show me the path of life:
    in thy presence is fulness of joy."*

But where is full joy when
    we are ill,
    we lose our jobs,
    our children disappoint us,
    our friends hurt us:

*Psalm16:11 KJV

they move away,
get sick,
some of them betray us,
they die,
and leave us bereaved—
and life is not just a rollicking adventure?
Life does get strenuous.
But in the middle of dissatisfaction,
disillusionment,
even disaster,
we can experience joy.
Not light, simpering,
superficial,
frivolous,
whimsical joy,
but deep-down inward,
constant
inexplicable
bountiful
imperishable joy.
God's joy—a heart attitude.
Money won't buy it.
We can't, and don't, inherit it—from an earthly estate.
It is God's gift to us.
His joy
changes barren,
bleak,
empty people
into beaming,
gleaming,
authentic followers
who know that God

cannot,
and will not
make a mistake.
Don't wait—until your pain disappears,
the tears stop falling,
your stomach stops hurting,
the lump in your throat dissolves,
and you can breathe freely again—
to experience his joy;
that might be a long time coming.
Change the way you look at,
feel about
the happenings in your life,
and when you have no joy of your own,
ask for his.
His joy overflows
and fills our empty places
until—we want no more.
Open your empty soul
to
his plenty—
he will fill it with
joy—that shall remain—
his joy.

Days of Glory

In the last several days
I have answered my phone to hear things like:
    "My daughter is pregnant—she's not married."
    "My marriage is in big trouble."
    "I have a serious eating disorder."
    "My doctor has ordered me to take a two-month sick leave."
    "I need open heart surgery."
    "My husband is unfaithful."
Many of us are going through
        difficult,
        even life-endangering situations
that seem to have no end.
It is almost impossible to believe
the inspired words of the apostle Paul:
"Our light affliction, which is but for a moment,
worketh for us a far more exceeding and eternal weight of glory."*
In these words, Paul
gives each of us
    a strong note of comfort,
    a message of assuring hope

*II Corinthians 4:17 KJV

for the trying times
that are too much
and too many for this life.
The purpose of those who know God
is to do something worthwhile,
accomplish our God-given tasks,
make the world a better place.
Adversity,
disappointment,
hopelessness
give us opportunities to
discover our potential
and realize his worth.
Paul and Silas—thrown into prison—
appeared to be failures.
Sorry,
dismal,
worthless.
Instead, these
dauntless,
courageous,
obedients
turned their prison cells
into a palace of praise
and a wonder of worship.
At midnight
there burst from those prison cells
songs of gladness,
shouts of thanksgiving
and victory.
They were heard by every prisoner
and echoed
by an earthquake.

It was from those dark prison days
that Paul gave us
lasting,
durable truths.*
If we can look failure full in the face,
see our best efforts come to nothing—
fall in ruins at our feet
—if we can see beyond them into
the unmarked,
uncertain future, and say,
"this light affliction
(regardless of how heavy it feels)
is for but a moment,"
then we can know that
the blood of spiritual royalty
washes through our veins
and we are born to
triumph.

*See Acts 16:19-40

A New Easter

Dawn was beginning to
push away the darkness of night.
Morning had not yet come.
Wide awake,
I carefully,
  quietly
slid out of bed,
fumbled in the blackness
for the clothes
I had laid out the evening before.
Dressing as quickly as the dim light permitted,
I slipped out the door into the shadowy
streets of Jerusalem.
The street lights revealed the starkened
trees,
whipped by winds from nearby Judea.
I didn't feel the chilling effect
of the twisting wind
or of the raw spring dampness
that permeated the early morning air.
This day had taken on a
different quality,
more exciting than any of the others,

immune to something as inconsequential
as weather.
I was on a secret mission—
My early morning trek to the place
where they laid my Lord!
It was as though I had gone back
almost two thousand years.
The words from the Gospel of Mark
filled my mind:
"And very early in the morning, the first day of the week,
  they came
unto the sepulchre at the rising of the sun."*
It was quiet as I scurried down deserted streets,
past row after row of darkened houses.
I tried to experience the feelings
of Mary—
            heartbroken,
            confused,
            wondering
as she walked
this same dark
    and lonely,
        shadowy path
to the garden tomb near Mount Calvary.
    I wondered what overwhelmed her most—
the loneliness,
the grief—the numbness beyond it,
the waiting,
and all of the "what nows."
Tears—my tears
began to fall

*Mark 16:2 KJV

as I felt
    the hot desolation
of Mary's pain still there through the many years.
The Easter atmosphere was electric,
    charged with emotion,
    pregnant with power,
as I walked the dark and lonely road
close to the place called
Calvary.
The knowledge that I would find
an empty tomb
only added strength to my strong feelings
of tender melancholy
as I thought of his suffering.
Quietly,
    reverently,
but not reluctantly,
I stepped into the empty tomb,
    sat on the roughly hewn stone,
and wept
    hot,
      searing,
        cleansing tears
as I contemplated the agony of my Lord.
    His agony—my agony.
I do not know;
    I cannot recall
how long I sat weeping
        and remembering.
I only know
    an angel came
and asked, as Jesus had so long ago,

"Woman, why are you weeping?
    Who have you been looking for?
He is not here.
    He is risen.
        HE is risen!"
How can I describe the ecstasy,
    the exultation,
    and the exhilarating joy
that filled me?
Hope sprang to life.
    Faith became reality
as my heart responded to the words:
"He is not here!
    HE is risen!
And HE is alive
forevermore!"
. . . and so am I!